Raw Food

How and Why to Succeed at Being a Raw Vegan

By: Kevin Kerr

Copyright © 2015 by Kevin Kerr - All rights reserved.

In no way is it legal to reproduce, duplicate, or transmit any part of this document in either electronic means or in printed format. Recording of this publication is strictly prohibited and any storage of this document is not allowed unless with written permission from the publisher.

The information provided herein is stated to be truthful and consistent, in that any liability, in terms of inattention or otherwise, by any usage or abuse of any policies, processes, or directions contained within is the solitary and utter responsibility of the recipient reader. Under no circumstances will any legal responsibility or blame be held against the publisher for any reparation, damages, or monetary loss due to the information herein, either directly or indirectly.

The information herein is offered for informational purposes solely, and is universal as so. The presentation of the information is without contract or any type of guarantee assurance.

You should consult your physician or other health care professional before making any lifestyle or nutritional changes that are discussed, in order to determine if the suggested practices are right for your needs.

4 Raw Food Recipes

Table of Contents

Why to Be Raw......................(p.6)
How to Succeed.....................(p.12)
Smoothies............................ (p.20)
Juices............................... (p.47)
Desserts........................... (p.77)
Soups.............................. (p.121)
Dressings & Sauces...............(p.141)
Salads.........................(p.162)
Wraps............................ (p.169)
Fermented Foods...................(p.174)
Gourmet Recipes...................(p.178)

Why to Be Raw

Digestion starts with the first bite of food as digestive enzymes are released to begin the process of breaking down the carbohydrates we eat. These are called amylases and they break down carbohydrates into glucose. The food then travels to the first half of our stomach where the carbohydrates are completely broken down. Once this is done it then moves to the second half of the stomach where pepsin (enzyme that breaks down proteins into amino acids) and hydrochloric acid are excreted. After this it moves into the small intestine where the majority of the fat you have eaten will be digested.

Raw food is any plant food that isn't heated over 118 degrees so that the precious digestive enzymes aren't destroyed. If I could pick one word to explain the reasoning behind eating an all raw vegan diet, primarily based on fruit, it would be without a doubt ENZYMES! In order for food to digest it must be broken down by digestive enzymes in order for our bodies to convert it into energy. Your body can only produce so many in this lifetime. From puberty and on the body produces 10% to 13% less enzymes every decade. Calorie restriction and fasting greatly influences these numbers in a positive manner. Enzymes are produced by the salivary glands when and if you chew your food, the stomach, the pancreas, the small intestine, and the 3 pounds bacteria in our bodies that weigh the same as our brain.

Enzymes are made up of amino acids just as proteins are. They are defined as protein catalysts and are biologically active meaning they contain energy. When an enzyme is taken orally it expends all of its energy clearing the blood of undigested food until all of its life force is used. There are two different types that are produced by the body which are digestive and metabolic. Metabolic enzymes are produced in the body and used for biochemical reactions, detoxification, and metabolic energy within the cells. An example would be the conversion of alpha-linoleic acid (ALA) omega 3 fatty acids and omega 6 linoleic acid (LA) to EPA and then DHA which comprises over 20 percent of the dry weight of the brain. This is done by metabolic enzymes produced by the body and shows the importance of eating a diet rich in enzymes and maintaining as close to a 1 to 1 balance of omega 3 fatty acids and omega 6 fatty acids as possible.

On average, 70% of the body's energy is used towards digestion, maintaining alkalinity of the blood and acidity of the stomach, and the continual production of digestive enzymes. The remaining systems of the body including the immune, respiratory, reproductive, cardiovascular, nervous, and muscular use the remaining percent. This is so important to understand because it proves how excessive eating devoid of enzymes drains our energy and leaves the body more susceptible to invading bacteria, fungus, parasites, and viruses which lead to disease. I can honestly say that I have experimented with nearly every supplement and superfood known to man at this current time and if I had to choose one it would be a balanced full spectrum enzyme blend designed to thoroughly break down fats, carbohydrates, and proteins. There have been claims that digestive enzymes are destroyed by the acidity of the stomach and don't make it into the intestine or bloodstream. However, recent discoveries through scientific study have shown that digestive enzymes become inactive in acid and become once again active in a more suitable ph. such as the blood. Our bodies are designed around this innate enzyme intelligence. It will only produce enough enzymes to digest the food that is consumed. When people are overweight it is a sign that they are eating more food than their body can handle which leaves undigested fats, carbs, and proteins in the blood leaving food for unwanted invaders. In short, digestive enzymes, taken in supplement form or in raw food, break down food so that your body doesn't have to manufacture them thus allowing you to have more energy which will in turn enable you to live a longer life.

When you cook food it produces a toxic compound called acrylamide which has been known to cause cancer, and studies have shown that when you ingest cooked food it stimulates the immune system to neutralize and get rid of it. Not to mention it destroys vitamins C, B1 (thiamine), B5 (pantothenic acid), B6 (pyridoxine), and B9 (folate). If you are going to cook the best way to preserve nutrition is by steaming for 5 minutes or less.

 Science has discovered that our bodies can only produce so many enzymes in this lifetime which is the number one reason to eat as much raw food as you enjoy. There are three ways that digestive enzymes are produced which are by plants, by our body, and by the 400,000 to 800,000 bacteria that live in our digestive tract. Our gut microflora or bacterial colonies adjust to our diet. Up to 15% of the calories from your food from your food are extracted by the bacteria in your colon and used to fuel you. Studies have conclusively shown that people who are overweight have less gut bacteria so the best way to replenish them by making fermented foods and repopulate your already existent colony by eating fruit!

 Our bodies are made of 30 trillion human cells and 100 trillion bacterial and fungal cells that reside on every square inch square inch out our bodies. A recent study had revealed that each person contains about 2 million different genes for bacteria and 23,000 for your cells meaning that only 1% of your body is you. Bacteria are fascinating, some deadly, but they do wonders for this planet and our bodies. Scientists believe they were the first living species on this earth. Bacteria in the gut are literally capable of producing protein by converting atmospheric nitrogen into amino acids, convert vitamin K to K2, manufacture all the B vitamins, and even synthesize vitamin B12 from the mineral cobalt. To me, it doesn't make much sense to eat meat from animals, considering we are ourselves flesh, because along with it you must have bacteria in our body to help digest and eliminate flesh. One last benefit of raw living foods I want to touch on before moving on to how to succeed on the diet is biophotons. Scientists have recently started learning about biophotons in raw foods which are essentially transmissions of light. Just like our bodies, plant foods give off light which transfers to us when we eat them. The foods with the highest biophoton emissions are wild, followed by organic and then conventional. They can also test people's radiation of biophoton light. Average people who eat a diet of junk food emitted around 1,000 units whereas those who ate healthy emitted around 83,000 units. This goes to show the importance of foraging and seeking out the cleanest foods you can find because once a food is picked it begins to lose its enzymes. Freezing and refrigerating lowers enzyme activity by 10%, but soaking and sprouting nuts and seed increases enzyme and vitamin content drastically. Everything that can be eaten raw should be eaten raw for the sake of the planet and respect of body.

How to Succeed

    My motto is eat less and love more! All the longest lived people in the world eat very little. The centenarians of Okinawa, Japan thrive on a low calorie (typically 1800 or less), low protein (40 grams or less), low fat, high carbohydrate, nearly 100% vegan diet based on sweet potatoes. The people in the Andean highlands of Ecuador and the Hunzas from northeast Kashmir live on similar starch-based diets and their oldest members live until they are 140 still limber into their old age. About a week ago a lady from Japan just died after having her 117th birthday. On the day she simply said, "I'm so happy." Right now there is a man in China who is 116 and woman in Mexico who is 127 years old right now and contributes her longevity to chocolate. There was an herbalist in China named Li Ching-Yuen who lived to be very old but I won't get into that. He lived on very powerful herbs and rice. Although longevity has a lot to do with reducing stress, breathing, and sunlight I also believe diet has a lot to do with it as well. It all starts with the right mindset.

    When on a vegan or vegetarian diet most people ask, "Where do you get your protein?" I tell them to go ask a hippo, horse, rhino, cow, kangaroo, gorilla (which are nine times stronger than humans), elephant, or raw vegan tortoise that lives to be 150 years old. Some long-lived whale or parrot might be able to answer your question better than I can I tell them. I'm kidding but there is protein, fat, and carbohydrates in every plant food. In all seriousness spirulina has 12 times more protein than beef ounce for ounce. Science tells us that there are 20 amino acids that make up the protein found in our bodies and that there are 9 essential ones that need to be obtained from diet. Goji berries actually contain all 20 amino acids. Complete proteins are considered to be the ones that contain all essential amino acids and on a raw vegan diet these include nuts, seeds, green leafy vegetables, chlorella, spirulina, hydrilla, and marine phytoplankton. I believe the healthiest way to thrive on this diet is to base it off of high quality fruits and enjoy overt fats and protein in moderation. Excess protein, refined carbs, and fats have been shown to cause nearly all of the diseases and cancers we are plagued with in today's day and age. Believe it or not our brains have evolved from eating fruit and it shows due to the evidence of the bigger cranial capacity of ancestors that lived 2 million years ago. They had bigger brains than we do today and we know this because of the studies done with primates. The species that eat more fruit have bigger brains. Fruits contain proteins, fats, carbs, vitamin, minerals, and steroid blocking compounds with delay the onset of puberty thus allowing the brain to develop longer and the organism to live longer.

Strive to eat mono meals, three times a day or less, as often as possible to ensure proper assimilation, nutrient absorption and elimination. Eating bigger meals less frequently throughout the day allows the body to heal and utilize the food you eat more efficiently. Opt for wild and organically grown heirloom foods; try adding dandelions to salads, smoothies or juices. The whole plant or herb I should say is edible, very nutritious, and medicinal. However, finding wild foods or affordability of organic is not always possible so here is a list of fruits and vegetables with the lowest pesticide content: asparagus avocados, bananas, broccoli, carrots, cabbage, eggplant, grapefruits, kiwi, mangoes, mushrooms, pineapple, romaine lettuce, sweet peas, sweet potatoes, and watermelon. I highly recommend that all other produce you consume is organically grown.

Aside from tasting better, being better for your body, and being cruelty-free; uncooked vegan food takes less prep time. The easiest way to succeed and thrive on this diet or true radiant health in general is to surround yourself with an abundance of the highest quality fruits that you can find. Don't worry about getting too many bananas because once they are ripe you can peel them and put them in bags and store them in the freezer where they will good for many months. You can use them for smoothies or for making ice cream by blending them with other fruits, raw cacao powder, or vanilla.

Eating foods that are high in resistant starch ensures that you feed the bacteria in your colon, so that they don't start climbing your intestines looking for food, which studies have shown to be very helpful for weight loss. The bacteria in turn produce short chain fatty acids that provide eventually provide fuel the cells once it is converted into glucose. This can be done by eating cooked and cooled starches, raw potatoes, unripe bananas or cashews.

Give your gut bacteria time to adjust to your new plant-based diet, and if you want to speed up the process then you can consume raw apple cider vinegar, take probiotics, and east a small amount of fermented foods every day. Fermenting fruits, vegetables, nuts, seeds, mushrooms and herbs can be as simple as cutting or blending them up and putting them in mason jars with water and salt. Let the jars sit out for several days or longer depending on the taste you enjoy. Be sure to try them periodically and when you find a taste you like put the jars in the refrigerator where they will remain good for many months. You can add raw apple cider vinegar or a capsule of probiotics to speed up the fermentation process. Superfoods can also be added for more nutritional value! I found it funny when I learned that bacteria, fungus, and algae have been in competition since on this planet since the beginning of its time because I consume all three on a daily basis and I believe you should too for optimal health, especially medicinal mushroom teas!

Before we get to the recipes I just want to say thank you for reading this far and now I'm going to give you all the knowledge I wish I would have known before adopting a raw food lifestyle. Eat a salad once a day with some sort of fat to increase the absorption of fat soluble vitamins and phytochemicals around lunch time because this is when your body can best metabolize fat, and always rotate your greens to ensure different nutrient profiles and to avoid oxalates from the same plants. Green plants are the most nutrient dense foods ounce for ounce but they produce these oxalates as a type of defense mechanism. To prevent any kind of buildup of oxalates in the body, which can block the absorption of important minerals, avoid eating copious amounts of the same green for months at a time. By all means don't avoid eating greens all together because you'd be missing out on an abundance of nourishment including chlorophyll which is one of the closest natural substances to human blood. Chlorophyll cleans your blood of any kind of contaminants and actually contains oxygen! I eat at least a half a pound of greens a day and sometimes one or two. The easiest way to get a lot of greens in your diet is through blending or juicing with a masticating juicer.

The more diverse your diet is in terms of variety and color the healthier you are going to be. There have been over 5,000 phytochemicals that have been discovered, and we just keep learning more about the wondrous benefits of plants. Be sure to include, melons, berries tropical fruits, all types of vegetables, and incorporate herbs into your diet daily. If you enjoy broccoli florets in your salad but don't enjoy eating the stalk raw save it and use it in your juices or salad dressings because it's full of calcium. Eat apple seeds even though they contain arsenic, to get sick from it you would have to eat many cups of them in one sitting. They contain vitamin B17 which many people have used to cure different types of cancer. It can also be in apricot seeds without the arsenic. For vitamin B12 eat fermented foods, nutritional yeast and hydrilla verticillata. For those that think you can't get enough B12 on a vegan diet you're very wrong because this is the highest source on the planet, and it's also the highest source of calcium. Not only this but it's high in lysine which is an amino acid that some people say vegan diets are deficient in. Always soak your nuts and seeds to lessen the amount of phytic acid which blocks the absorption of certain minerals. Our bodies actually produce it but too much is counterproductive. Fruit is fuel and it contains little to no natural toxins. Don't be scared to eat 10 bananas, 5 mangoes, or 6 apples for one meal if you're hungry enough.

Lastly, I want to talk about superfoods and supplements you may want to consider. Anyone that lives in the northern hemisphere of the world needs to be supplementing with vitamin D3 vegan or not. The sun's rays don't provide us with enough sunlight for our body to convert in these regions, especially in the winter time. Periodically be sure to include greens, pumpkin seeds, cashews, sunflower seeds, almonds, and most definitely chlorella to ensure proper zinc levels. I also recommended a brazil nut day to maintain adequate selenium levels and highly encourage consuming sea vegetables such as kelp or nori periodically for the abundance of iodine they contain to maintain radiant health. If you want to supplement with omega 3 fatty acids in the form of DHA and EPA then I suggest a brand called Ovega because it is grown indoors making it very clean and they test it for purity. It provides the most product and costs the least amount. It can be found at vitacost.com for the lowest price I have found. If you want to include DHA and EPA in your diet in a whole food then look no further than marine phytoplankton (nannochloropsis gaditana) powder. Although it is very pricey it is the most nutrient dense food on the planet. If you want to start enjoying the benefits of enzymes then I recommend getting a 1000 count bag from puradyme.com which is the best available deal. The man who started the company is 63 and has been a raw foodist for over 40 years. He used raw foods and enzymes to cure himself of a brain tumor when he was 21. The crazy thing is that he actually looks like he's 40 years old. Well that's all I have to say for now. Peace is with you!

Smoothies

Spearmint Lemon Balm Blend

- 10 lemon balm leaves
- 10 spearmint leaves
- 2 bananas
- ½ cup cherries
- ½ cup blueberries
- 2 brazil nuts
- small handful of walnuts
- 1 tsp. Maca powder
- small pinch of sea salt
- 2 cups of water

Blend and enjoy!

Serves: 1 or 2.

Smooth Melon Treat

- 3 cups of cantaloupe
- 4 bananas
- 3 cups of spinach
- 2 cups of water

Blend and enjoy!

Serves: 1 to 3.

Kaleicious
- 2 cups of kale
- 3 peaches
- 1 cup of black raspberries
- 2 cups of coconut milk
- 2 tsps. of acai berry powder

Blend and enjoy!

Serves: 2.

Swiss Bliss
- 2 cups of swiss chard
- 2 apples
- 1 cup of blueberries
- 1 banana
- 1 cup of cilantro
- 2 cups of coconut water
- 1 tsp. lucuma powder

Blend and enjoy!

Serves: 2.

Bodybuilder
- 1 cup soaked raw quinoa
- 3 bananas
- ¾ cup wild blueberries
- 2 stalks of kale
- small pinch of pink Himalayan salt
- 2 cups of water

Blend and enjoy!

Serves: 1.

Yellow Beauty
- 10 ginkgo biloba leaves
- 2 bananas
- 1 inch slice of fresh pineapple
- juice from ½ a lemon
- 2 cups of coconut water

Blend and enjoy!

Serves: 1 or 2.

Mango Melon Blend
- 3 cups of watermelon
- 3 cups of honey dew
- 1 mango
- 2 cups of water

Blend and enjoy!

Serves: 1 or 2.

Raw Vegan Milkshake
- 3 bananas
- ½ inch slice of fresh pineapple
- 1 tsp. maca powder
- 1 tbsp. coconut oil
- ½ tsp. camu camu berry powder
- 2 brazil nuts
- 1 tsp. olive oil
- pinch of sea salt
- 2 tbsps. raw cacao powder for a chocolate milkshake or 2 vanilla beans for a vanilla milkshake. Add both for twist. :)

Blend and enjoy!

Serves: 2.

Berrychaga
- One gallon of cold wild chaga tea
- 4 ounces of blueberries
- 4 ounces of blackberries
- 4 ounces of red raspberries
- ⅓ cup of hemp seed oil
- 1 handful dates

Blend and serve!

Serves 3 to 6.

Chagadate
- One gallon of cold wild chaga tea
- 14 ounces of dried pitted dates
- 3 tbsps. maple syrup

Blend and share!

Optional add ins: 5 bananas and/or 3 tbsps. of organic maple syrup.

Serves: 3 to 6.

Chaga Banana Surprise
- 2 cups cold wild chaga tea
- 1 or 2 ataulfo mangos
- 2 bananas
- 2 tbsps. coconut oil
- 1 tsp. maca powder
- 1 tsp. moringa powder
- 1 tsp. camu camu berry powder

Blend and enjoy!

Serves: 1 or 2.

Liver Lover
- two cups dandelion leaves
- two large oranges
- 1 pear
- 1 avocado
- 1 tsp. cinnamon powder

Blend and enjoy!

Serves: 2.

Chocolate Smoothie

- 2 tbsps. raw cacao powder
- 10 cacao beans
- 2 tsps. mucuna pruriens powder
- 1 tbsps. raw cacao butter
- 4 tsps. maple syrup
- 2 cups of spring water

Optional add ins:
- fulvic minerals
- chaga mushroom extract or mycelium powder
- reishi mushroom extract or mycelium powder
- pine pollen
- shilajit

Blend and enjoy!

Serves: 1 or 2.

Green Mint Jackfruit Smoothie
- 2 cups coconut water
- 4 chunks frozen jackfruit
- 1 leaf swiss chard
- ½ inch slice fresh cut pineapple
- 4 to 7 fresh mint leaves
- 2 tsps. noni powder
- 1 tsp. maple syrup

Blend and enjoy! Serves: 2.

Red Wonder
- 2 cups coconut water
- ½ cup goji berries
- 4 cups strawberries
- 1 banana
- 2 tsps. maple syrup

Blend and enjoy! Serves: 2.

Beautiful Morning
- 2 cups spring water
- A handful of spinach
- ½ large or 1 whole avocado
- ½ cup strawberries
- ½ cup red raspberries
- ½ cup blueberries

Blend and enjoy! Serves: 2.

Berry Ferry
- 1 ½ cups spring water
- 2 ounces blueberries
- 2 ounces blackberries
- 3 ounces red raspberries
- 3 ounces strawberries

Blend and enjoy! Serves: 1 or 2.

Tropical Concoction
- 1 ½ cups coconut water
- 1 inch slice of fresh pineapple
- 1 mangoe
- 1 peeled kiwi

Blend and enjoy! Serves: 1 or 2.

Juiced Smoothie
- 2 oranges
- 2 grapefruits
- 2 bananas
- 1 tsp. camu camu berry powder
- ⅓ cup goji berries

    First, juice the oranges and grapefruits, then blend together with the rest of the ingredients and enjoy!

Serves: 1 or 2.

A Good Date
- 2 handfuls of your favorite variety of dried pitted medjool dates
- 3 cups of spring water
- 6 drops of vanilla extract

Blend and enjoy!

Serves: 1 or 2.

The Right Side of the Bed
- Juice of 7 navel oranges
- blend juice with 1 large banana or 2 small bananas

Optional add ins:
- Vitamin D capsule
- Your favorite berries
- A handful of greens
- A quarter chunk of beetroot

Blend and enjoy!

Serves: 1.

Classic
- Your choice of 2 or 3 bananas
- 2 hefty handfuls of your favorite greens
- 3 cups Spring water

Optional Add ins:
- Dried Mulberries
- Raw organic Acai Berry Powder
- Dried Papaya
- Dried Jackfruit

Blend and enjoy!

Serves: 1.

Tropical Delight
- 1 Cup of fresh Pineapple
- 1 Cup of fresh Mango
- 2 Whole Mangosteens (white flesh) (if not available substitute with coconut meat)
- 3 cups of coconut water

Blend and enjoy!

Serves: 1.

Scrumptious Easy Meal
- juice 1 lb. of carrots
- juice ½ lb. of your favorite greens
- juice 3 valencia oranges

Blend juice with with the following ingredients:
- 2 bananas
- 10 whole shelled pecans
- 2 tbsp. of coconut oil
- ⅓ tsp. of camu camu berry powder
- ½ tsp. wild harvested cold extracted mucuna pruriens powder
- 1 tsp. of wild harvested cold extracted ginseng powder

Blend and enjoy!

Serves: 2.

The Three Musketeers
- 1 lemon (peel and all if organic)
- ½ cup of soaked chia seeds
- 2 tbsp. of raw organic expeller-pressed coconut oil
- 3 cups of spring water or your favorite warm herbal tea

Optional add ins:
- 1 tsp. maca root powder
- 1 tsp. raw cacao powder
- 1 tsp. mesquite powder

Blend and enjoy!

Serves: 1 or 2.

Superfood Smoothie
- 10 goji berries
- 10 golden berries
- 1 tsp. of camu camu berry powder
- 1 avocado
- 2 cups of pineapple
- gel from a fresh aloe vera leaf
- 3 cups of spring water

Blend and enjoy!

Serves: 2.

Too Good

- 2 tbsp. of raw cacao powder
- 10 cacao beans
- 2 bananas
- 2 tbsp. of your favorite nut butter
- 2 tsp. of maple syrup
- 3 cups of spring water

Optional add ins:

- fulvic Minerals
- chaga mushroom extract or powder
- reishi mushroom extract or powder
- pine pollen powder
- shilajit powder

Blend and enjoy!

Serves: 1 or 2.

Fruit Heaven
- 2 cups coconut water
- 1 large mango
- 2 bananas
- 1 kiwi
- 2 tbsps. coconut oil
- 1 tsp. lucuma powder
- 1 tsp. camu camu berry powder

Blend and enjoy!

Serves: 1 or 2.

Purple Delight
- 1 ½ cups spring water
- 1 cup blackberries
- 2 bananas

Blend and enjoy!

Serves: 1.

My Main Romaine
- 2 cups romaine lettuce
- 2 cups of grapes
- 1 cup parsley
- 2 cups of pineapple
- 1 tsp. spirulina
- 1 tsp. chlorella
- 2 cups of almond milk

Blend and enjoy!

Serves: 2.

Holy Bok Choy
- 2 cups bok choy
- 1 tsp. holy basil powder
- 1 tbsp. hemp seeds
- 2 bananas
- 1 tbsp. goji berries
- 1 tbsp. of golden berries
- 2 cups of water

Blend and enjoy!

Serves: 2.

Pop My Collard
- 2 cups collard greens
- 2 mangoes
- 1 tsp. marine phytoplankton
- 1 tsp. ground vanilla
- 1 tbsp. flax seeds
- 1 tbsp. baobab powder
- 2 cups cashew milk

Blend and enjoy!

Serves: 1 or 2.

Fruit Juice Slushie
First juice the following fruits:
- 1 cup red raspberries
- 1 mango
- 1 pineapple
- 1 small papaya or ½ large papaya
- 2 kiwis

Blend juice with ice and enjoy!

Serves: 1 or 2.

Islander

First juice the following fruits:
- 2 medium guavas
- 2 cups strawberries
- 1 mango
- 1 pineapple
- 2 apples

Blend with 3 bananas and serve!

Serves: 3.

Grapefruit Delight

First juice the following fruits:
- 4 large grapefruits
- 3 small oranges

Blend with 2 bananas, 1 cup of your favorite greens and serve!

Serves: 2.

Beet Root Detox

First juice the following ingredients:
- 2 beets
- 1 head of broccoli
- 1 sweet potato
- 1 cup of cabbage
- 2 apples

Blend with the following ingredients:
- 2 tsps. MSM powder
- 2 bananas
- 1 tbsp. goji berry powder
- 10 drops of fulvic acid
- 1 tsp. shilajit
- 1 tsp. stevia powder
- 2 capsules of probiotics

Serve and enjoy with a loved one!

Pearlicious Green Drink
- 2 pear
- 3 cups spinach
- 2 tbsp. almond butter
- 1 cup blueberries
- 1 cup strawberries
- 1 tsp. green coffee bean extract
- 1 tbsp. raw cacao powder
- ½ tsp. cinnamon

Blend and enjoy!

Serves: 1 or 2.

A Drink of Heaven
- 5 bananas
- 1 tsp. ashwagandha extract
- 1 tsp. amla extract
- 1 tsp. bacopa extract
- 1 tsp. tribulus extract
- ½ tsp. turmeric extract
- 2 tbsps. hemp protein powder
- 2 cups coconut milk

Blend and enjoy!

Serves: 2.

Mulberry Moringa Blast
- ½ cup dried mulberries or 1 ½ cups fresh
- 2 tsps. moringa powder
- 1 tsp. nettle powder
- 1 thumb-sized chunk of ginger
- 3 bananas
- 2 cups bok choy
- 2 cups of water

Blend and enjoy!

Serves: 2.

Cucumber Delight
- 1 large cucumber (skin and all if organic)
- ½ lemon (skin and all if organic)
- 1 apple
- 1 banana
- 1 cup romaine lettuce
- 1 cup cilantro
- two cups of water

Blend and enjoy!

Serves: 1 or 2.

Apricot Elixir
- 4 pitted apricots
- ½ cup macadamia nuts
- 2 cups kale
- 1 cup wild blueberries
- 1 cup cherries
- 1 banana
- 2 cups almonds milk

Blend and enjoy!

Serves: 1 or 2.

Pomegranate Passion
- 2 cups seeds and fruit
- 4 bananas
- ½ cup pili nuts
- 1 tbsp. chia seeds
- 1 tsp. vanilla powder
- 1 squeeze of fresh lime juice
- 2 cups water

Blend and enjoy!

Serves: 2.

Magnificent Morning
- 2 cups kale
- 1 cucumber
- 2 stalk celery
- 1 cup mint
- 2 apples
- 1 cup parsley
- 2 carrots
- 1 orange
- 3 cups pineapple
- 2 cups water

Blend and enjoy!

Serves: 1 or 2.

Banana Cashew Goddess
- 2 tbsp. cashew butter
- 2 bananas
- 1 tsp. cinnamon powder
- 2 cups water

Blend and enjoy!

Serves: 1 or 2.

Tomato Treat
- 1 large tomato
- 2 oranges
- 2 cups strawberries
- 1 banana
- 3 cups cantaloupe
- ½ cup sunflower seeds
- 1 tsp. kelp flakes
- 2 cups hemp seed milk

Blend and enjoy!

Serves: 2.

Papaya Perfection
- 2 cups papaya
- 2 cups swiss chard
- 1 apples
- ½ cup sacha inchi seeds
- 2 cups water

Blend and enjoy!

Serves: 2.

Blueberry Blast
- 4 cups blueberries
- 2 cups kale
- 1 apple
- 2 cups watermelon
- 1 cup pineapple
- 2 cups coconut water

Blend and enjoy!

Serves: 1 or 2.

Skin Savior
- 1 cup blueberries
- 1 cup black raspberries
- 1 cup red raspberries
- 1 banana
- ½ cucumber
- 1 cup spinach
- 1 cup water

Blend and enjoy!

Serves: 1 or 2.

Kiwi Delight
- 2 peeled kiwis
- 1 avocado
- 1 tsp. chlorella
- 1 tsp. spirulina
- ½ tsp. marine phytoplankton
- 1 tsp. stevia powder
- 2 cups water

Blend and enjoy!

Serves: 1.

Lovable Lunch
- 3 stalks celery
- 1 cucumber
- 1 apple
- 1 tbsp. coconut oil
- 1 banana
- 2 cups strawberries
- 1 tbsp. flax seeds
- 2 cups almond milk

Blend and enjoy!

Serves: 2.

Juices

Sweet Surrender
- 1 pineapple
- 7 gala apples
- 7 blood blood red oranges
- 1 lemon
- 3 stalks swiss chard

Healer
- 4 stalks celery
- 1 small beet (including greens)
- 1 pound lacinto kale
- ½ pound carrots
- 1 red delicious apple

Deep Green
- 3 cups spinach
- 4 stalks celery
- 2 leaves swiss chard
- 2 stalks broccoli
- 1 golden delicious apple
- 1 bartlett pear
- thumb-sized chunk of ginger root

Summertime Heaven
- ¾ parts watermelon(s)
- ¼ part pear(s)

Skin Healer
- 3 grapefruits
- 2 mangoes
- ½ beet
- ½ lemon

Liver Detox
- 3 beets
- 4 oranges

Nourisher
- 2 leaves swiss chard
- 2 cups strawberries
- 1 apple of choice
- 1 medium-sized cucumber

Green Powerhouse
- 4 stalks celery
- 4 stalks kale
- 3 leaves romaine lettuce
- 1 medium-sized cucumber
- 10-20 mint leaves
- ginger root
- ½ lemon (peel and all if organic)

Refreshing Cleanse
- 5 stalks celery
- 2 cups grapes

Simple Treat
- 2 pounds carrots
- 2 inch slice of a fresh whole pineapple

Juiced Love
- 7 stalks kale
- 2 cups strawberries
- 1 medium-sized apple
- 1 medium-sized cucumber

Carrot Beet Fast
- 5 pounds carrots
- 1 beet
- 3 tsps. organic maca powder
- 2 tsps. ceylon cinnamon powder

Juice vegetables, then stir or shake in the maca and cinnamon. The results yield a delicious drink that will satisfy your body all day!

Sweet Greens
- 4 cups spinach
- 1 apple
- 2 large carrots

Sweet Celery Juice
- 10 stalks celery
- 2 pears
- ginger root

Red Heaven
- 1 beet
- 2 sticks rhubarb
- 1 red bell pepper
- 1 apple
- 1 pear
- 2 carrots
- ginger root

The Usual
- 3 pounds of carrots
- 1 beetroot
- ½ of a Lemon

Summertime Delight
- 4 pounds of watermelon
- 2 pears
- 1 whole lime
- 1 peach

Green Dream
- 10 leaves of your favorite kale
- 4 stalks of celery
- 1 whole cucumber
- 2 of your favorite organic apples
- 10 stalks of cilantro
- A handful of blueberries
- A handful of blackberries

Breakfast and Lunch
- 1 grapefruit
- 15 cranberries
- 2 oranges
- ½ of a mango
- 1 inch slice of a fresh pineapple

Woah
- 3 handfuls of Strawberries
- 2 handfuls of Red Raspberries
- 1 persimmon
- 2 Asian pears
- 4 cups concord grapes
- 2 bunches

Juiced Love
- 4 kiwis
- 5 peaches
- 1 lime
- 6 stalks of rainbow swiss chard
- 1 cucumber

Chlorophyll Central
- 1 pound of spinach
- 10 stalks of kale
- 1 cucumber
- 3 stalks of celery
- 8 kiwis

Passionate Pomegranate
- 3 pomegranates (Seed and all) (Not the shell or white flesh inside)
- 4 passion fruits
- 1 head of romaine Lettuce
- 1 beetroot
- 1 lemon

Longevity in a Cup
- 15 carrots
- 1 beetroot
- ½ of a lemon
- 10 cranberries
- 1 whole head and stalk of broccoli
- 5 leaves of kale

Natural Tang
- 10 carrots
- 7 oranges
- 2 mangos
- 5 peaches
- sliver of a habanero pepper
- 1 inch chunk of ginger root

Skin Lover
- 1 pound of carrots
- 1 large cucumber
- 2 stalks celery

Tropical Delight
- 1 guava
- 1 papaya
- 1 pineapple
- 1 orange
- 1 mango

Magnificent Melon
- ½ of a cantaloupe
- 3 carrots
- 1 apple
- 1 orange
- 1 grapefruit

Cucumber Carrot
- 1 pound of carrots
- 2 cucumbers

Real Good Morning
- 2 or 3 carrots
- 1 apple
- ½ of a beet
- 1 pint of strawberries

Sensational Start
- ½ of a pineapple
- 1 orange
- 1 cup of strawberries
- 1 bunch of red grapes
- 1 bunch of parsley

Pineapple Delight
- 1 whole pineapple
- 2 oranges
- 1 bunch of cilantro
- 1 bunch of mint

Lemon Ginger Elixir
- 1 lemon
- 1 thumb-sized chunk of ginger
- 8 ounces of spinach
- 2 apples
- 1 bunch of parsley
- 1 bunch of cilantro
- 1 cucumber

Liver Cleanser
- 1 apple
- 1 beet
- 1 pound of carrots
- 2 lemons
- 2 pears

Lemelon
- 4 cups watermelon
- 1 cucumber
- 1 lemon
- 1 lime

Cucumber Cleanse
- 2 or 3 cucumbers
- 1 pound of carrots
- 1 apple
- 1 grapefruit

Mint Melon
- 1 bunch of mint
- 1 stalk of celery
- 1 cucumber

Berry Blast
- 1 cup blackberries
- 1 cup strawberries
- 1 cup raspberries
- 1 cup blueberries
- 1 head of your favorite greens
- 3 cups watermelon

Carrot Turmeric Apple
- 1 pound of carrots
- 2 apples
- 1 thumb-sized of turmeric

Mango Love
- 1 mango
- 3 kiwis
- 2 or 3 carrots

Early Morning
- ½ pineapple
- 1 mango
- 1 tomato
- 3 stalks swiss chard
- ½ lemon
- 1 sweet potato
- 3 stalks celery

Hawaiian Treat
- 1 papaya
- 1 guava
- 1 pineapple
- 1 pound of rambutans
- 1 pound of lychee

Perfect Papaya
- 1 papaya
- 1 pineapple

Melonator
- ½ cantaloupe
- ½ cantaloupe
- ½ watermelon
- 2 cucumbers

Perfect Sunrise
- ½ pineapple
- 2 mangoes

Peachy Pear
- 3 peaches
- 2 pears

Detoxer
- ½ pineapple
- 1 orange
- 1 papaya
- 1 mango
- 2 or 3 carrots
- ½ lime
- ½ lemon
- 1 bunch of your favorite greens

Beelieve It
- 1 beet
- 3 or 4 carrots
- 2 oranges
- 1 cucumber

Green Carrot
- 2 pounds of carrots
- 2 bunches of parsley

Rainbow Morning

- ½ cucumber
- 1 yellow bell pepper
- 1 tomato
- 1 orange
- 4 ounces of spinach
- 3 stalks celery
- 2 or 3 carrots

Blueberry Grapple

- 1 lemon
- 1 cup blueberries
- 1 cup red grapes
- 1 apple

Mexican Juice

- 1 large red bell pepper
- 2 stalks of celery
- ½ lime
- 6 stalks of cilantro
- 1 apple

Spicy Tomato
- 1 tomato
- 3 carrots
- 2 stalks of celery
- 1 thumb-sized chunk of ginger
- 1 thumb-sized or horseradish root
- 5 stalks of cilantro
- 2 radishes
- 1 clove of garlic

Pearfect Grape Juice
- 3 pears
- 2 cups of your favorite grapes

Pineapple Punch
- 2 cups of pineapple
- 1 pint of strawberries
- 1 mango

Crazy Cantaloupe
- 1 cantaloupe
- 3 pears

Stress Reducer
- 4 stalks celery
- ½ fennel bulb
- ½ head of romaine lettuce
- ½ pineapple

Perfect Peppermint
- 1 cup of peppermint leaves
- 3 oranges
- 3 apples

Apple Ginger Juice
- 5 apples
- 1 lemon
- 1 thumb-sized chunk of ginger

Skin Lover
- 1 cucumber
- 1 bunch of parsley
- 1 apple
- 3 or 4 carrots

Red Glory
- 1 beet
- 1 tomato
- 1 red bell pepper
- 1 cucumber
- ½ pound of carrots
- 3 leaves of red cabbage

Natural Punch
- 3 cups kale
- 2 cups parsley
- 2 cups spinach
- 1 apple
- 4 stalks celery
- 1 orange bell pepper

Paradise
- 1 papaya
- 2 oranges
- ½ pineapple
- 1 lime
- 1 thumb-sized chunk of ginger

Islander
- 1 pineapple
- 1 pint strawberries
- 2 apples
- 1 papaya

Melon Ginger
- 1 thumb-sized chunk of ginger
- 1/2 cantaloupe
- 1 pint strawberries
- 1 orange

Crafty Cabbage
- 1 thumb-sized chunk of ginger
- 2 stalks celery
- 5 leaves of cabbage
- 1 yellow bell pepper
- 1 pear

Quick Breakfast
- 1 cantaloupe
- ½ pound of carrots
- ½ lemon
- 1 apple

Fat Buster
- 4 carrots
- 3 stalks celery
- 1 cucumber
- 1 small bunch of cilantro
- 1 beet
- 1 apple

Kiwi Passion
- 1 passion fruit
- 1 cup grapes
- 2 kiwis

Cranberry Pear Juice
- 3 pears
- 1 peach
- 2 cups cranberries
- ½ pineapple

Ravishing Red Raspberry
- 2 pints red raspberries
- 2 oranges
- 1 lime

Fabulous Forager
- 1 head purple cabbage
- 2 cups red grapes
- 2 cups blueberries
- 4 stalks kale

A Taste of the Forrest
- 1 bunch of cilantro
- 1 bunch of parsley
- 5 stalks of kale
- 1 beet
- 1 cucumber
- 1 lemon
- 1 thumb-sized chunk of turmeric
- 1 thumb-sized chunk of ginger

Revitalizer
- 3 apples
- 3 stalks celery
- 1 cucumber
- 1 lime
- 1 thumb-sized chunk of ginger

Lonely Veggie
- 3 oranges
- 1 apple
- 1 pear
- 1 cucumber
- 1 zucchini

Green Delight
- 5 stalks kale
- 5 stalks swiss chard
- 1 cucumber
- 1 apple
- 1 orange
- 7 clementines

Citrus Twist
- 1 cucumber
- 1 lemon
- 1 lime
- 3 kiwis
- 2 apples
- 1 thumb-sized chunk of turmeric

Berry Pearific
- 4 pears
- 3 cups watermelon
- 1 pint black raspberries

The Melon Musketeers
- 3 cups watermelon
- 3 cups honeydew
- 3 cups cantaloupe
- 1 cucumber

Summer Treat
- 1 pint strawberries
- ½ pineapple
- 3 cups red grapes

Berry Good Treat
- 1 cup cranberries
- 1 cup strawberries
- 1 cup raspberries
- 1 cup blueberries
- add to 1 cup of filtered or spring water

The Motivator
- 4 stalks of celery
- 1 cucumber
- 4 ounces of spinach
- 1 apple
- 1 orange bell pepper

Kool Kiwi
- 3 kiwi fruits
- ½ pineapple
- 1 orange
- 1 thumb-sized chunk of turmeric

Peachy Apricot
- 2 peaches
- 2 apricots
- 1 pear
- 1 apple

Spicy Orange
- 1 thumb-sized chunk of ginger
- 3 oranges
- ½ honeydew
- ½ lime

Perfection
- 1 tomato
- ½ red leaf lettuce
- 3 stalks celery
- 1 carrot
- 1 yellow red bell pepper

Tangy Berry
- 1 pint strawberries
- 1 pint red raspberries
- 1 lemon
- 1 pound of spinach

Cranberry Apple Juice
- 1 pint of strawberries
- 1 apples

Love Elixir
- 1 peach
- 2 cups of red grapes
- 2 cups of strawberries
- 1 apple

Ravishing Rainbow
- 3 stalks celery
- 3 carrots
- 1 cucumber
- 1 yellow squash
- 1 apple

Ultimate Vegetable Juice
- 2 carrots
- 2 stalks celery
- 1/2 beet
- 1 small bunch of parsley
- ½ head of lettuce
- 1 small bunch of watercress
- 2 ounces of spinach
- 3 tomatoes
- sea salt to taste

Tropical Love
- 1 orange
- 1 pineapple
- 1 mango
- 1 papaya
- 1 guava

Papple Pear
- 2 apples
- 2 pears
- ½ pineapple

Body Lover
- 2 cups grapes
- 2 large oranges
- 2 lemons

Citrusy Grape
- 2 cups of grapes
- 3 oranges
- 1 lemon

Ginger Melon
- 1 thumb-sized chunk of ginger
- 3 cups watermelon
- 3 cups cantaloupe

Green Heaven
- 4 ounces of spinach
- 1 head of broccoli
- 3 apples
- 1 lemon

Fast Morning
- 3 apples
- 3 pears
- 3 oranges

Apple Pie
- 4 cups butternut squash
- 3 apples
- 1 tsp. of cinnamon powder

V5
- 3 tomatoes
- 5 leaves of cabbage
- 1 bunch of parsley
- 3 stalks of celery
- 1 cucumber
- 1 thumb-sized chunk of turmeric
- salt and pepper to taste

Sweet Intention
- 1 sweet potato
- 3 carrots
- 1 beet
- 1 bell pepper
- 1 pear
- 1 apple
- 1 orange
- ½ head bok choy

Desserts

Chocolate Avocado Pudding

- 1 medium-sized avocado
- 3 tbsps. maple syrup
- 3 tbsps. raw cacao powder
- pinch of pink Himalayan salt

Blend until smooth and serve! Top with cacao nibs, goji berries, golden berries, mulberries, or hemp seeds.

Serves: 2.

Durian Ice Cream

- 1 pound durian
- 1 tbsp. maple syrup
- 3 drops peppermint oil
- 1 tsp. spirulina
- ¼ cup cacao nibs
- ¼ cup hemp seeds or milled macadamia nuts

Blend or process the durian, honey, peppermint, and spirulina until smooth. Sprinkle on the toppings and enjoy your mint chocolate chip ice cream!

Serves: 1 to 3.

Orange Macadamia Pudding

- 2 peeled oranges
- 1 cup Macadamia nuts
- 1 cup dates
- 1-2 tbsps. liquefied coconut oil
- 1 tsp. dried lavender flowers

Blend all the ingredients until smooth. If it is too thick, add the juice of another orange or two. Scoop into small, single serving dishes and leave in the fridge overnight.

Serves: 3 to 5.

Berry Pudding

- 1 banana
- handful frozen strawberries
- handful blueberries
- 3-5 pitted dates
- 1/4 tsp. sea salt
- 1/2 tsp. cinnamon
- 1/2 tsp. vanilla
- 2 tbsps. cacao
- 1/4 cup non-dairy milk
- 1 tbsp. cashew butter

Blend and enjoy!

Serves: 2

Maple Ice Cream

- 2 frozen bananas
- 1-2 tbsps. maple syrup
- 1/4 cup walnuts
- dash of cinnamon, to taste
- dash of nutmeg, to taste

Blend the bananas and maple syrup until smooth, in a food processor.

Add in the walnuts and spices, to taste. Blend and enjoy!

Serves: 1 or 2.

Brownies and Caramel Sauce

- 1 cup raw cacao powder
- 1 cup walnuts
- 1 cup pecans
- ¼ cup hemp seeds
- ¾ cup dried pitted dates
- 1 tsp. maple syrup
- ¼ tsp. sea salt

Using a food processor or high speed blender, mill and mix the ingredients until a thick batter-like consistency is reached. Put your brownie mix into a container, or form into individual treats. They are delicious without the sauce, but mixing the following ingredients in a blender will provide you with the perfect raw caramel sauce!

- 1 tbsp. raw cacao powder
- 1 tsp. mesquite powder
- 1 tsp. lucuma powder
- 4 tsps. maple syrup
- 1 tsp. organic maple syrup
- 1 tsp. coconut oil

Blend well, top brownies, and enjoy! Serves: 3 to 6.

Raw Chocolate Nut Butter Cookies

- 1 cup of your favorite raw nuts or seeds
- ½ cup of your favorite raw nut or seed butter
- ½ cup dried pitted dates
- 2 tbsps. raw cacao nibs
- 2 tbsps. maple syrup
- 2 tbsps. coconut oil

Blend or process all the ingredients until a cookie dough consistency is reached. Form into your desired shapes and refrigerate for at least one hour. Next, place the following ingredients in a bowl and dip each cookie.

- 3 tbsps. liquefied coconut oil
- 3 tbsps. raw cacao powder
- 2 tbsps. maple syrup

Serves: 2 to 4.

Raw Fig Cookies

- 2 pound raw figs
- 1 cup hemp seeds
- ½ cup macadamia nuts
- 2 tbsps. maple syrup
- ¼ tsp. sea salt

First process or blend figs and set aside. Next, process or blend ½ cup hemp seeds, macadamia nuts, and salt. Add the rest of the hemp seeds, and mix together with a spoon. Form figs into desired shapes and cover with the milled nuts and seeds! ENJOY!

Serves: 4 to 10.

Chocolate Chip Cookies

- 1/2 cup raw organic walnuts
- 1/2 cup raw organic cashews
- 1 cup of your favorite variety of pitted dates
- 6 drops vanilla extract or ½ tsp. dried vanilla bean powder
- 4 oz of your favorite organic chocolate bar
- 1 tsp. maca powder

Blend or process all of the ingredients. A tbsp. of water may be necessary depending on how dry the dates are. This can be prevented by soaking them for 2 hours prior to making the recipe.

Form into cookies, Enjoy!

Makes about 5 to 7 servings.

Oatmeal Raisin Cookies

- 2 cups raw organic oats
- 1 cup raw pecans
- 1/2 cup firmly packed grated fresh apple (about 2 medium apples)
- 1 cup dried raisins
- 1/2 cup pitted dates
- 4 Tbsps. organic liquefied coconut oil
- 3 tbsps. coconut sugar
- 1 tsp. ground cinnamon
- 1/2 tsp. ground ginger
- 1 tsp. alcohol free vanilla extract
- 1 tbsp. freshly grated lemon zest
- pinch sea salt

Directions:

1. Add the pecans into a food processor fitted with the S blade, and a few times until roughly chopped. Empty them into a mixing bowl.
2. Place the oats in the food processor with the cinnamon, ginger, vanilla, sweetener, and sea salt and pulse a few times until well combined.
3. Add in the dates, apple, lemon zest, coconut oil and pulse again.
4. Transfer this mixture to a large bowl and fold through the remaining ingredients until a thick clustered "dough" forms.
5. Tweak the flavors to taste. You might want

more sweetener, cinnamon or lemon zest.
6. Form this dough into medium sized cookies and place on mesh dehydrator sheets.
7. Dehydrate cookies in your dehydrator at 100 degrees for 12 - 15 hours or more depending on your preference.
8. This recipe yields 12 medium-sized dense chewy cookies. Alternatively, you could make 24 smaller cookies.

Note: For those of you without a dehydrator, you can try making these oatmeal cookies in a conventional oven by preheating your oven to 300 F, placing the cookies in, closing the oven door, turning the oven off and allowing it to cool with the cookies inside. The cookies should have a nice chewy texture.

Mulberry Kiwi Bars

- 1 ½ cups dried mulberries
- 2 cups dried figs
- 2 cups pitted dates
- 2 tsp. of freshly ground cinnamon

Directions:

Place all ingredients in the food processor and pulse until the
mixture reaches an even consistency. Take out the mixture, and press it into a glass bowl to form it. When ready, remove it and slice into bar chunks to make your energy bars. Now it's time to make the kiwi topping!

Ingredients for the Cherry Drizzle:

- 2 cups pitted cherries
- 1 cup pitted dates

Directions:

Blend both ingredients until desired consistency is reached! Dip energy bars in mixture and refrigerate for an hour! Enjoy!

Serves: 4

Chocolate Macadamia Nut Cookies

- 2 cups organic raw macadamia nuts
- ½ cup raw organic cacao powder
- 2 tbsps. liquefied organic coconut oil
- ½ cup organic raw agave or maple syrup
- 2 tsp organic vanilla extract
- ½ tsp sea salt

Directions:

1. Place the macadamia nuts in the food processor and pulse a few times until coarsely ground.
2. Now add in the cacao powder and pulse a few times until the consistency of bread crumbs.
3. Add in all of the other ingredients and pulse until well combined. The mixture should form a ball.
4. Take this ball and roll it out to about a 1/4 inch on parchment paper.
5. Now cut out even small circles. I used the top of a shot glass.
6. Place these circles on dehydrator sheets and slowly warm at 115 degrees for 48 hours.
7. Store in a sealed container in the fridge for about 3 weeks.

Serves: 5

90 Raw Food Recipes

Enjoy!

Gingerbread Cookies

- 2 cups of your favorite raw flour
- 1 ½ cups pitted dates
- ⅛ tsp. sea salt
- ½ tsp. vanilla powder
- 2 tbsps. fresh ginger
- 1 tsp. cinnamon
- 1 tsp. nutmeg
- 1 tbsp. molasses
- ¼ cup maple syrup
- 2 tbsps. liquefied coconut oil

Directions:

Place all the ingredients in a food processor or blender and mix until even consistency is reached. Form into cookies and enjoy!

Serves 4 to 8.

Chocolate Pumpkin Brownies

- 1 pie pumpkin
- 2 ½ lbs. pitted dates
- 3 ripe persimmons
- ½ raw cacao powder
- 1 tbsp. cinnamon
- 1 cup raw organic pecans
- 1 cup dried black mission figs
- 1 Tbs. pumpkin spices (nutmeg and clove)
- 1 thumb-sized chunk of ginger
- 1 small vanilla bean

Directions:

Add everything to your high speed blender and blend until even consistency is reached. Form into brownies and enjoy!

Serves 5 to 7.

Oreos

- ½ cup almonds
- ¼ cup ground flax or chia seeds
- ¼ cup raw cacao powder
- ¼ cup shredded coconut
- 1 tbsp. maple syrup
- 1 tsp. vanilla extract

For the stuffing:

- ¼ cup cashews
- 2 tbsps. shredded coconut
- 2 tbsps. liquefied coconut oil
- 1 tbsp. honey or maple syrup
- 1 tsp. vanilla extract

Directions:

Blend the almonds and flax meal in a food processor until the almonds are a powder.

Add in the cacao, shredded coconut, sweetener and vanilla. Blend until the dough starts to stick together. You may need to add a splash of water.

You can either roll the dough out into a cylinder and cut the cookies that way or roll out the mixture and use a cookie cutter. I opted for the latter and used the lid from a bottle that was the perfect size. Make sure to have an even number of oreo halves at the end!

Place them in a dehydrator overnight or if you

don't have one you can refrigerate.

Now it's time to do the filling! Blend up all of the ingredients in a food processor.

Sandwich the filling between the cookies and enjoy!

Serves: 4 to 6.

Chocolate Truffles

- 1 cup pitted dates
- ¼ cup hemp hearts for the recipe and a little extra for rolling truffles in
- 1 heaping tbsp. of cacao powder and a little extra for rolling truffles in

Directions:

Blend the dates, hemp hearts and cacao in a food processor until the mixture sticks together. If your dates are super moist, you could even do this by hand in a bowl if you don't have a food processor.

Roll the mixture into balls.

Roll the truffles in some cacao powder, hemp hearts, leave them plain or all of the above!

Enjoy!

Serves: 2 to 4.

Almond Butter Cups

- ¼ cup liquefied coconut oil
- ¼ cup raw organic cacao powder
- 1 tsp. maple syrup
- 2 tbsps. almond butter

Directions:

Mix cacao powder and sweetener of choice in with coconut oil in a small bowl.

Fill 6 little paper cupcake cups with about a tsp. of the chocolate in each.

Place in freezer for 5 minutes or until hardened.

Put a dollop of almond butter in each cup.

Cover with the remaining chocolate.

Freeze for another 5 minutes or until hardened.

Enjoy!

Serves: 3 to 4.

Raw Chocolate
- 4 ounces raw organic cacao butter
- 3 ounces raw organic coconut oil
- 4 to 6 tbsps. raw organic cacao powder
- 2 tsps. cinnamon
- Coconut sugar, lo han guo, goji berry, lucuma, maple syrup, cane sugar, stevia, schizandra berry, or yacon. You decide! I recommend lo han guo, stevia, or maple syrup for chocolate.

First, melt the cacao butter and coconut oil in your double-broiler system at the lowest temperature possible to save nutrients. Next, stir in the cacao powder, cinnamon and sweetener until you get consistent "chocolate syrup". Pour into a plate or silicone molds and put into the refrigerator until it hardens up. It usually only takes an hour or less. Break into pieces or free from molds and enjoy! :)

Optional: If you want to get creative you can add dried fruits before you refrigerate such as dates, goji berries or mulberries. If you really want to make things interesting and healthy try adding nuts or seeds, nut butters, or superfood powders!

Chocolate Caramel Bars

- 2 cups raw almonds
- 1 ½ cups pitted dates
- splash of vanilla extract

Caramel:
- 1 cup pitted dates
- 1 tbsp. liquefied coconut oil
- ¼ cup water
- splash of vanilla extract
- pinch of sea salt

Chocolate:

- 2 tbsps. liquefied coconut oil
- ¼ cup raw cacao powder
- 2 ½ tbsps. maple syrup
- pinch of sea salt

Directions:

Blend the almonds into flour in your food processor.

Add in the dates and vanilla and blend until it sticks together.

Press this base mixture into a 9" x 9" pan, that's lined with parchment paper or cling wrap so that you can easily pull it out at the end to slice it.

Blend all of the caramel ingredients in your food processor until creamy. Add a tbsp. or two of water if needed.

Spread the caramel on top of the base and place in the freezer while you mix up the chocolate.

Mix up all of the chocolate ingredients in a small bowl.

Spread the chocolate over the caramel.

Let the squares set in the freezer overnight.

Pull the squares out of the pan, slice them and ENJOY!

Serves: 4 to 6.

Fudge

- 2 pounds of pitted medjool dates
- 8 ounces of raw cashew butter

Blend together, form in a pan, cut into squares, top with goji or golden berries, and serve!

Fit for 3 to 5 people!

Lemon Coconut Bars

Base:

- ¾ cup oats
- ¾ cup dates
- ¾ cup coconut shreds

Lemon layer:

- ⅓ cup melted coconut oil
- ¼ cup maple syrup (or 1 cup pitted dates)
- juice from 3 lemons
- ½ cup shredded coconut
- 2 medium bananas

To make the base: pulse the oats or buckwheat groats and coconut shreds in your food processor until they become a rough flour. Add the dates and process until it all sticks together. Press into the bottom of a square baking pan and put in the fridge.

To make the lemon layer: blend all the ingredients until smooth. See if you like the taste and adjust accordingly. Spread evenly on to the base layer and set in the fridge overnight. The next day, cut into squares and sprinkle with finely ground coconut flakes and enjoy!

Serves: 5 to 7.

Raw Apple Apricot Cobbler

- 8 peeled and cored apples
- 4 sliced and quartered apricots
- ¼ cup organic maple syrup
- 3 tbsps. liquefied coconut oil
- 1 tsp. cinnamon
- ¼ tsp. sea salt

Mix all the ingredients except for the apricots in a blender or food processor until an even consistency is reached, then mix in the chunks of apricots but keep them whole. This will be used as the filling to this delicious dessert. Now it's time to make the shell and topping.

- 1 cup walnuts
- 1 cup dried pitted dates
- 3 tbsps. coconut oil
- 2 tsps. cinnamon
- 1 ½ tsps. vanilla extract or 1 vanilla bean

Mix the ingredients in a food processor or blender until an even chunky consistency is reached. Pour into a pyrex pie crust but save enough for the topping. Top and serve! Fit for ten people. If you desire it warm you can heat at the lowest temperature possible in your oven or dehydrator for 20 minutes to several hours.

Serves: 4 to 6.

Watermelon Cake

- 1 watermelon
- 1 cup soaked hemp seeds
- 1 cup soaked cashews
- ½ cup coconut water
- 1 juiced lemon
- 2 vanilla beans
- 3 tbsps. raw honey
- ½ cup soaked almonds

Start by peeling the watermelon and shaping it to your desired size of cake(s). (Cup cakes are also possible.) Next, blend or process the rest of the ingredients until smooth. Cover the entire watermelon. Process the almonds and stick them to the sides of your cake. Top with your favorite fruits and refrigerate for an hour!

Serves: 3 to 6.

Carrot Cake

Macadamia Nut Frosting:
- 1 ½ cups macadamia nuts
- juice from 1 lemon
- 2 tbsps. liquefied coconut oil
- 2 tbsps. coconut sugar
- 1 tsp. vanilla powder
- 1 tbsp. water

Carrot Cake:
- 3 large carrots, peeled and chopped into small chunks or pulp from 6 large carrots that were juiced
- 1 ½ cups oats
- 2 cups pitted dates
- ½ cup dried coconut powder
- 1 tsp. cinnamon
- ½ tsp. nutmeg

Frosting:

Blend all ingredients in your high speed blender until smooth, adding water as needed. Put in the fridge for at least an hour before using.

Cake:

Process the oats into flour in your food processor then add the rest of the ingredients in and process until it begins to stick together. Put the mixture into a bowl to form it into your cake or simply construct it into your desired shape then put in the freezer until it's solid. Then simply frost your cake and you officially have the healthiest and most delicious carrot cake in the world! Enjoy!

Serves: 3 to 4.

Vanilla Cheesecake

Crust:

- 1 cup pitted medjool dates
- 2 cups raw almonds

Surround the inside of a cake pan with wax paper or plastic wrap. Pulse dates and nuts together in food processor until you get an even consistency. Form and press mixture into the bottom of the pan. Put in fridge for at least an hour before putting the cake together.

Cheesecake:

- 3 cups soaked raw cashews
- ¾ cup lemon juice
- ⅔ cup maple syrup
- ¾ cup liquified coconut oil
- ½ tsp. sea salt
- 1 tsp. vanilla extract
- 1 vanilla bean

Blend all ingredients, except coconut oil, together until smooth and creamy. Add coconut oil and make sure it blends completely. Pour onto crust in cake pan and set in the fridge for at least two hours. Take out of cake pan holding onto the wax paper or plastic wrap and put it on a plate.

Slice and enjoy!

Serves: 2 to 6.

108 Raw Food Recipes

Cinnamon Cake

Dough:

- 1 cup pecans
- ½ cup ground flax seeds
- ¼ cup maple syrup
- 3 tbsps. raw buckwheat flour
- 5 pitted dates

Filling:

- ½ cup pitted medjool dates
- ¼ cup water
- 2 tbsps. cinnamon
- 1 tbsp/ liquefied coconut oil
- ¼ tsp. sea salt
- 4 pitted medjool dates
- 2 tbsps. chopped hazelnuts

Icing:

- 1 cup cashews
- ¼ cup coconut oil
- 4 tbsps. fresh squeezed lemon juice
- 1 tbsp. maple syrup

Directions

- Mix all of the dough ingredients in a food processor until it starts sticking together until it forms a dough. Set aside.
- Mix all of the filling ingredients in a food processor or a blender until well blended.
- In a medium sized spring form pan or form your cake to the desired shape you want with your hands.
- Put in the freezer for about an hour to make it easier to apply icing.
- Mix all of the icing ingredients in a food processor or blend together until desired consistency is reached.
- Ice the cake!
- Top with cinnamon and your favorite chopped nuts.

Serves: 4 to 7.

Enjoy!

Mini Chocolate Cake

Crust:

- ⅓ cup pecans
- ⅓ cup pitted medjool dates
- 2 tsps. cacao powder

Filling:

- 1 avocado
- 1 tbsp. cacao powder
- 1 tbsp. maple syrup

Chocolate topping:

- 2 tbsps. liquified coconut oil
- 2 tbsps. cacao powder
- 1 tsp. maple syrup, or to taste.

Directions:

Blend the crust ingredients, using a food processor, and press the mixture down into a spring form cake pan.

Blend the filling ingredients, using a food processor, and spoon the mixture on top of the crust in the spring form pan.

Place the torte in the freezer while you make the chocolate topping.

Mix the chocolate ingredients in a small bowl.

Pour the chocolate sauce over top of the torte.

Freeze overnight and enjoy!

Serves: 1 or 2.

Coconut Cream Pie

Crust:
- 1 ½ cups nuts
- 1 ½ cups pitted medjool dates
- pinch of sea salt

Chocolate Cream:
- 2 avocados
- ⅓ cup maple syrup
- ½ tsp. cinnamon
- ¼ cup raw cacao powder
- 2 tbsps. mesquite powder
- 2 tbsps. liquefied coconut oil
- pinch of sea salt

Whipped Cream:
- 1 ½ cups of coconut milk
- 3 tbsps. raw coconut sugar
- 1 vanilla bean

Crust:

    Pulse nuts in food processor until they're the size of crumbs. Add dates and pulse until it lumps together. Feel free to add cinnamon, salt, vanilla or more sweeteners here. Press into your favorite pie pan and stick in the fridge.

Chocolate Cream:

Blend or process all ingredients until silky smooth. Now slice 3-4 bananas and put them on the bottom of the crust. Spoon on the chocolate cream and put on another player of banana slices. Set in the fridge again.

Right before serving, take out coconut milk from the fridge. Spoon off the thick fat from the top - you want this. Put the milk you spooned out into a mixing bowl with the sugar and beat until it turns into a cream! Spoon over your pie and enjoy!

Serves: 3 to 4.

Raw Pumpkin Pie

Crust:

- 1 cup cashews
- 1 cup almonds
- ¼ cup pitted medjool dates
- 1 cup dates
- ⅛ tsp. sea salt

Pumpkin Filling:

- 1 cubed pie pumpkin without the seeds
- 1 cup dates
- 4 tbsps. liquefied coconut oil
- ⅓ cup maple syrup
- 3 tbsps. pumpkin pie spices (cinnamon, nutmeg, ginger and cloves)

Crust:

Process the nuts in your food processor until they are like a rough flour. add the dates, raisins and salt. Pulse until it all sticks together in a lump. Press into the bottom of a pie dish and refrigerate.

Pie Filling:

Process the pumpkin cubes until they can't get any smaller in your food processor. Add in the other ingredients and process until it can't get any smoother. Transfer the filling to your high speed blender and blend on the highest setting until an even consistency is reached. Spread the filling onto your pie crust and let it set in the fridge for a few hours.

Serves: 3 to 6.

Citrus Coconut Cheesecake

Crust:
- 1 cup walnuts
- 1 cup almonds
- 1 cup pitted medjool dates

Lemon Layer:
- 3 cups cashews
- 1 cup coconut milk
- juice of 2 lemons
- 3 tbsps. maple syrup
- ½ tsp. sea salt
- 3 tbsps. liquefied coconut oil

Lime Layer:
- 1 avocado
- juice of 2 limes
- 3 tbsps. maple syrup
- 1 tbsp. coconut oil
- ⅛ cup coconut milk
- ¼ cup coconut flakes

Crust:

Blend all the ingredients in your food processor until it starts clumping together so you can press it into shapes. Press into the bottom of a spring form pan lined with plastic wrap. Put in fridge for at least an hour.

Lemon Layer:

Blend all ingredients together in your blender until creamy smooth. Pour half of it onto your crust and set aside the remaining half. Put back in the fridge for another hour.

Lime Layer:
Blend all ingredients until smooth in your food processor or blender. Tour all of this onto the first layer on the crust, then pour on the remaining lemon layer from earlier. Let it sit in the fridge for at least a few hours. Enjoy!

Serves: 4 to 6.

Chia Fruit Pie

Crust:

- ¼ cup pitted medjool dates
- ¼ cup raisins
- ¼ cup dried figs

Filling:
- 2 bananas
- 2 tbsp. chia or flax seeds

Topping:
- ¾ cup chopped strawberries
- ¾ cup chopped kiwi
- 1 medium-sized mango

To make the crust:

Put all the ingredients in your food processor and pulse until everything is in small pieces that stick together - don't process too much or it will be hard to work with. Press into an aluminum pie tin. Put in the fridge.

To make the filling:

Mash the banana with fork and then add the chia or flax seeds.

Assembly:

Take the crusts gently out of the tins. Spread the banana chia mix into the crusts and then top off with the fruit. Enjoy!

Serves: 3 to 4.

Soups

Herbal Green Pea
- 2 cups peas
- 1 avocado
- 1 ½ cups almond milk
- ½ cup fresh basil
- ½ small red onion
- ½ cup fresh chives
- 1 clove garlic
- sea salt to taste

Spicy Cucumber Cabbage
- 2 large cucumbers
- 3 cabbage leaves
- 1 (hot) pepper of choice
- 1 small heirloom tomato
- 2 tablespoons olive oil
- pink Himalayan salt to taste

Mexican Fiesta
- 2 medium heirloom tomatoes
- 2 red bell peppers
- 8 sun dried tomatoes
- 8 sprigs of fresh cilantro
- 2 stalks celery
- 1 cup water
- fresh squeeze lime juice
- ½ avocado
- 2 tbsp. cold-pressed olive oil
- 1 clove garlic
- ¼ tsp. cumin
- ½ tsp. chili or cayenne powder
- ½ teaspoon paprika
- sea salt to taste

Sea Soup Specialty
- 3 cups zucchini noodles made with spiralizer (add in whole after soup is blended)
- 3 nori sheets
- 1 tsp. dulse
- ½ tsp. kelp granules
- 2 tbsp. coconut oil
- 2 cups hot water or your favorite tea

Tomato Basil
- 3 medium heirloom tomatoes
- 4 sun dried tomatoes
- 2 stalks celery
- small chunk of red onion
- ½ clove fresh garlic
- 5 leaves fresh basil
- ½ avocado
- sea salt to taste

Cream of Cucumber
- 2 large cucumbers (peel and all if organic)
- ½ cup macadamia nuts
- squeeze of fresh lemon juice
- 1 clove garlic
- 1 avocado
- 1 cup of water
- sea salt to taste

Cream of Tomato
- 2 large heirloom tomatoes
- 3 stalks celery
- 1 medium carrot
- 1 clove garlic
- juice of 1 lemon
- ½ cup raw cashews
- 1 avocado
- 1 orange bell pepper
- 2 pitted dried medjool dates (optional)
- ½ tsp. cumin
- 5 sprigs cilantro
- 1 tbsp. soaked pumpkin seeds
- pink Himalayan salt to taste

Cream of Nectarine
- 7 to 8 peeled and pitted nectarines (depending on size)
- 2 cups spinach
- ½ cup water
- ½ tsp. cinnamon

Cream of Mango
- 3 cups fresh mango
- 1 cup coconut milk
- 1 tbsp. coconut cream
- 2 tbsp. coconut sugar
- 3 leaves fresh mint
- 3 leaves fresh spearmint

Cream of Carrot
- 2 large carrots
- 1 cup macadamia nuts
- 1 clove garlic
- 1 tbsp. raw apple cider vinegar
- 3 green onions
- 1 red bell pepper
- sea salt to taste

Green Goodness
- 1 cucumber (peel and all if organic)
- 1 cup spinach
- 1 orange bell pepper
- 1 avocado
- 1 tbsp. raw tahini
- juice of 1 lemon
- sea salt to taste

Fennel Basil Tomato Soup
- 1 fennel bulb
- 1 cup water
- 2 medium heirloom tomatoes
- ½ cup fresh basil
- ½ yellow bell pepper
- fresh squeeze lime juice
- sea salt to taste

Cream of Lime
- 2 avocados
- juice of 2 small limes (or 1 large)
- 3 sprigs fresh cilantro
- ½ cup fresh chives
- 1 tsp. cumin
- 1 stalk celery
- 1 cup water
- sea salt to taste

Cream of Celery
- 7 stalks celery
- ½ cup raw cashews
- 1 avocado
- 1 clove garlic
- 1 cup water
- kala namak salt to taste

Cream of Zucchini
- 3 cups zucchini (peel and all if organic)
- 1 cup peas
- 2 stalks celery
- 1 avocado
- 1 cup water
- juice of 1 lemon
- 2 cloves fresh garlic
- 1 tsp. fresh thyme
- 1 tsp. turmeric
- pinch of cayenne pepper
- sea salt to taste

Cream of Pumpkin
- 1 cup pumpkin (seeds and skin removed)
- 2 pitted dried medjool dates
- 1 cup raw cashews
- ¼ tsp. cinnamon
- sea salt to taste

Green Onion Tomato Soup
- 2 large heirloom tomatoes
- 1 yellow bell pepper
- 3 green onions
- 1 cucumber
- 1 clove garlic
- ½ small red onion
- sea salt to taste

Cream of Spinach
- 2 cups spinach
- 1 cup water
- 1 cup macadamia nuts
- 4 green onions
- 1 clove garlic
- ½ tsp nutmeg
- sea salt to taste

Carrot Ginger Soup
- 2 large carrots
- 1 thumb-sized piece of ginger
- 2 tbsp. black sesame seeds
- 2 pitted dried medjool dates
- pinch of black or cayenne pepper
- ½ tsp. turmeric
- 2 cups water
- sea salt to taste

Cream of Broccoli
- 1 head of broccoli (excluding stalk)
- 2 stalks celery
- 1 clove garlic
- ½ small red onion
- fresh squeeze lemon juice
- tsp. dried oregano
- 1 cup water
- pinch of black pepper
- ½ tsp turmeric
- kala namak salt to taste

Garden Blend
- 1 zucchini (peel and all if organic)
- 2 medium heirloom tomatoes
- 2 stalks celery
- 2 medium carrots
- 1 clove garlic
- 2 pitted dried medjool dates
- 1 cup water
- 2 tbsp. olive oil
- pinch of black pepper
- 1 tsp. turmeric
- sea salt to taste

Cream of Cauliflower
- 4 cups cauliflower
- 1 cup soaked raw almonds
- 1 tsp. olive oil
- 1 tsp. coconut oil
- 1 cup arugula
- ½ tsp. rosemary
- sea salt to taste

Strawberry Beet Soup
- 10 whole strawberries (including green tops)
- 2 small beets
- 2 cups water
- 3 green onions
- sea salt to taste

Spicy Lime Soup
- 1 stalk celery
- 1 cup yellow squash
- juice of 1 lime
- 1 chili pepper
- 2 medium carrots
- 2 small heirloom tomatoes
- 1 cup zucchini
- 1 cup cabbage
- 1 clove garlic
- 1 cup water
- sea salt to taste

Carrot Soup
- 1 whole head of broccoli
- 2 medium carrots
- 1 medium heirloom tomato
- ½ zucchini
- 5 raw brazil nuts
- 1 cup water
- sea salt to taste

Cream of Lemon
- 1 lemon (peel and all if organic)
- 1 small heirloom tomato
- 1 avocado
- ¼ cup olive oil
- ½ cup fresh parsley
- 4 stalks celery
- 1 tsp. maple syrup
- 3 cups water
- sea salt to taste

Cream of Mushroom
- 8 oz. of your favorite mushrooms
- 2 cups water
- 4 green onions
- ½ cup cashews
- ¼ cup pine nuts
- ¼ cup hazelnuts
- 4 sprigs fresh parsley
- sea salt to taste

Cream of Cabbage
- 2 cups cabbage
- 2 cups peas
- 1 avocado
- ½ zucchini (peel and all if organic)
- 1 stalk celery
- 1 tbsp. chia seeds
- ½ small red onion
- sea salt to taste

Cream of Pumpkin
- 2 cups pumpkin
- 2 cups water
- 2 cups cauliflower
- ½ cup pecans
- ½ tsp. mustard powder
- 1 tsp. cumin
- 3 sprigs cilantro
- sea salt to taste

Winter Specialty Soup
- 2 cups water
- 3 cups pumpkin
- 1 small carrot
- 2 green onions
- 1 stalk celery
- 1 cup kale
- 1 thumb-sized chunk of ginger
- 1 clove garlic
- 1 avocado
- 1 chili pepper
- sea salt to taste

Thai Ginger Soup
- 2 cups water
- ½ red bell pepper
- 1 small carrot
- 1 stalk celery
- 1 acorn squash
- 3 green onions
- fresh squeeze lemon juice
- 1 small apple
- ½ cup cashews
- 1 thumb-sized chunk of ginger
- 1 clove garlic
- 3 sprigs cilantro
- sea salt to taste

Cooling Watermelon Soup
- 3 cups watermelon
- juice of 1 lime
- 1 small cucumber (peel and all if organic)
- ½ cup fresh mint

Vegan Heaven Soup
- 2 cups water
- 2 cups broccoli
- 2 stalks celery
- 2 green onions
- ½ cup cashews
- 1 clove garlic
- 1 sprig fresh rosemary
- 1 sprig fresh lime
- sea salt to taste

Light Lettuce Soup
- ½ lb. romaine lettuce
- 2 cups peas
- 2 green onions
- 1 cup water
- sea salt to taste

Belly Buster Soup
- 1 small raw sweet potato
- 2 cups water
- 1 cup pumpkin
- 1 red bell pepper
- 1 stalk celery
- 1 medium carrot
- 1 green onion
- 1 small heirloom tomato
- 1 cup cabbage
- sea salt to taste

Cream of Pepper
- 1 red bell pepper
- 1 clove garlic
- 1 avocado
- 1 large heirloom tomato
- ½ small red onion
- 1 tsp. cumin
- sea salt to taste

Wonderland Soup
- 2 cups swiss chard
- 3 cups water
- 1 small carrot
- 1 stalk celery
- 2 green onions
- ½ cup brazil nuts
- 1 clove garlic
- squeeze of fresh lime juice
- ½ tsp. turmeric
- pinch of black pepper
- sea salt to taste

Cream of Chestnut
- 2 cups water
- ½ cup chestnuts
- 2 large carrots
- 1 stalk celery
- 1 sprig of parsley, rosemary and thyme
- 2 basil leaves
- sea salt to taste

Exquisite Tomato Soup
- 1 cup brazil nut milk
- 1 cup water
- 1 large heirloom tomato
- ½ cup sun dried tomatoes
- 1 red bell pepper
- 1 stalk celery
- ½ small red onion
- ¼ cup cashews
- 1 small carrot
- ¼ cup fresh basil
- 1 clove garlic
- pinch of cayenne pepper
- 1 tsp. oregano
- 2 tbsps. lemon juice
- sea salt to taste

Cream of Corn
- 2 cups raw corn
- ¼ cup cashews
- 1 cup water
- 1 clove garlic
- sea salt to taste

Dressings & Sauces

Raw Hummus

- ½ cup sesame seeds
- 1 zucchini
- ½ cup tahini
- 2 tablespoons cold-pressed olive oil
- 1 to 2 tablespoons lemon juice
- 1 clove garlic
- ½ red bell pepper
- 1 or 2 red chillies
- sea salt to taste

Peel the zucchini. Put the sesame seeds in your blender and blend until nearly powdered. Add remaining ingredients and blend until smooth. Serves with raw vegetables, raw crackers, or use as a dressing for your salad or wrap!

Fresh Dill Dressing

- 2 tbsps. raw apple cider vinegar
- 1 tbsp. lemon juice
- 1 tbsp. diced red onion
- 2 tbsps. chopped fresh dill
- 1 avocado
- pinch of black pepper
- ½ tsp. turmeric
- sea salt to taste

Dressing of Love

- ½ cup soaked macadamia nuts
- ¼ cup pine nuts
- 2 pitted dried medjool dates
- 6 basil leaves
- 1 clove garlic
- ½ cup coconut water
- 1 tsp. hydrilla powder
- 1 tsp. marine phytoplankton powder
- 1 tsp. chlorella powder
- 1 tsp. spirulina powder
- sea salt to taste

Pink Panda
- 1 cup soaked sunflower seeds
- 1 cup cauliflower
- 1 chunk of beet root
- 1 tablespoon hemp seed oil
- 1 medium heirloom tomato
- 1 medium carrot
- squeeze of lime juice
- sea salt to taste

Good Green Finishing
- 5 grape leaves
- 1 cup broccoli
- ½ cup fresh chives
- 1 avocado
- 1 tablespoon olive oil
- ½ cup fresh cilantro or parsley
- 1 tsp. moringa powder
- 1 tsp. marine phytoplankton powder
- 1 tsp. hydrilla verticillata powder
- kala namak salt to taste

Satisfactory Sauce

- 1 nori sheet
- 1 avocado
- 1 tsp. sacha inchi oil
- 1 tsp. sesame seed oil
- 1 medium tomato
- handful of soaked almonds
- 1 broccoli stalk
- 1 tsp. bentonite clay
- 2 cloves garlic
- pink Himalayan salt to taste

Spicy Orange Sauce

- 1 avocado
- 1 medium cucumber
- 1 orange bell pepper
- 1 medium carrot
- 1 habanero pepper
- chunk of red onion
- sea salt to taste

Healing Sauce
- handful of soaked macadamia nuts
- 1 avocado
- 1 cup crimini mushrooms
- 1 clove garlic
- 1 cup broccoli
- 1 tsp. olive oil
- 1 small carrot
- 1 medium heirloom tomato
- small chunk of onion
- squeeze of fresh lemon juice
- sea salt to taste

Peppy Pepper Sauce
- 1 red bell pepper
- ½ small red onion
- ½ avocado
- 1 tbsp. hemp seed oil
- kala namak salt to taste

Creamy Celery Almond Dressing
- 3 stalks celery
- 1 cup soaked almonds
- 1 large heirloom tomato
- 3 cloves garlic
- 1 tbsp. olive oil
- pinch of sea salt

Skin Nourisher
- 1 large cucumber
- handful of soaked walnuts
- squeeze of fresh lemon
- 2 cloves garlic
- 2 tbsp. raw apple cider vinegar
- 1 tsp. hemp seed oil
- 1 tsp. bentonite clay
- 1 tsp. maca powder
- 2 probiotic capsules
- pink Himalayan salt to taste

Raw Mayonnaise
- 1 cup soaked raw cashews
- ¼ cup fresh cauliflower
- 1 to 2 dried pitted medjool dates
- squeeze of fresh lemon juice
- ¼ cup cold-pressed olive oil
- 1 tsp. raw apple cider vinegar
- ¼ cup water
- sea salt to taste

Raw Ketchup
- 1 ½ cups fresh diced heirloom tomatoes
- ½ cup sun dried tomatoes
- 1 to 2 dried pitted medjool dates
- ¼ cup cold-pressed olive oil
- 1 tbsp. raw apple cider vinegar
- sea salt to taste

Raw Mustard

- ⅓ cup water
- ¼ cup yellow mustard seeds
- ¼ cup brown mustard seeds
- ¾ cup raw apple cider vinegar
- 1 to 2 dried pitted medjool dates
- ½ tsp. turmeric
- sea salt to taste

For "honey" mustard add ½ cup maple syrup or more!

Raw Barbeque Sauce

- 1 cup soaked sun dried tomatoes
- 5 tbsp. raw apple cider vinegar
- ½ tsp. liquid smoke
- 1 clove garlic
- 2 tbsp. chopped red onion
- ¼ cup maple syrup
- 1 ¼ cup water
- juice of ½ lemon
- sea salt to taste

Raw Hot Sauce
- 4 oz. of your favorite hot peppers
- 1 cup raw apple cider vinegar
- 3 cloves garlic
- ½ tsp. chili powder
- 4 sprigs cilantro
- ¼ tsp. cumin
- juice of ½ lemon
- sea salt to taste

Raw Vegan Pesto
- 2 cups fresh basil
- ½ cup walnuts or macadamia nuts
- ½ cup olive oil or 1 avocado
- 3 tbsp. nutritional yeast
- 1 tbsp. fresh lemon juice
- sea salt to taste

Nacho Cheese
- ½ cup soaked sunflower seeds
- ½ orange red bell pepper
- 3 tbsp. nutritional yeast
- 2 tbsp. fresh lemon juice
- 5 tbsp. warm water
- sea salt to taste

Lime Avocado Dressing
- 1 avocado
- 2 tbsps. olive oil
- 2 tbsps. lime juice
- juice of 1 orange
- 1 green onion
- 1 small habanero pepper
- sea salt to taste

Mango Mustard
- 1 cup fresh mango
- 2 tsps. tahini
- 2 tbsps. raw mustard
- 1 tsp. raw apple cider vinegar
- 2 tbsps. water
- sea salt to taste

Italian Dressing
- ¼ cup olive oil
- ¼ cup chia or flax oil
- 6 tbsps. lemon juice
- ¼ cup raw apple cider vinegar
- ½ tsp. oregano
- ½ tsp. onion powder
- ½ tsp. dry basil
- 2 cloves garlic
- sea salt to taste

Thyme Sunflower Dressing
- ½ cup soaked sunflower seeds
- ¼ cup fresh thyme
- ½ tsp. dried basil
- ¼ cup water
- 2 tbsps. lemon juice
- 2 tbsps. olive oil
- ¼ tsp. kelp granules
- sea salt to taste

Raw Thousand Island
- 1 medium heirloom tomato
- ⅓ cup raw tahini
- 2 tbsps. raw apple cider vinegar
- pinch of cayenne pepper
- sea salt to taste

Mix in finely diced raw pickles after blending!

Spinach Walnut Sauce
- 3 cups spinach
- 1 clove garlic
- ½ cup walnuts
- ¼ cup water
- 1 tbsp. lemon juice
- 1 tbsp. olive oil
- ¼ tsp. nutmeg
- ¼ tsp. rosemary
- sea salt to taste

Creamy Pepper Dressing
- ½ cup cashew milk
- ⅓ cup raw apple cider vinegar
- 1 clove garlic
- 1 tsp. pink peppercorns
- 1 tsp. white peppercorns
- ½ tsp. onion powder
- 2 tsps. chia seeds
- sea salt to taste

Red Pepper Sauce
- 2 tbsps. pili nut butter
- 1 tbsp. lemon juice
- ¼ cup stone ground mustard
- 1 red bell pepper
- 1 clove garlic
- sea salt to taste

Raw Vegan Ranch Dressing
- 1 cup soaked cashews
- ¼ cup olive oil
- 3 tbsps. lemon juice
- ½ cup hemp seed milk
- 2 cloves garlic
- 1 tsp. dried dill
- 2 tbsps. fresh parsley
- ½ tsp. onion powder
- sea salt to taste

Almond Ginger Dressing
- ½ cup soaked almonds
- ½ cup almond milk
- 1 cup water
- 4 tbsps. raw tahini
- 6 pitted dried medjool dates
- 1 clove garlic
- 1 thumb-sized chunk of ginger
- sea salt to taste

Lemongrass Dressing
- 1 lemongrass core
- ¼ cup pumpkin seed butter
- 3 tbsps. raw apple cider vinegar
- 2 tsps. coconut sugar
- ⅓ cup water
- dash of cayenne pepper
- sea salt to taste

Lemon Tahini Dressing
- ½ cup raw tahini
- ⅓ cup lemon juice
- ¼ tsp. onion powder
- ¼ cup water
- sea salt to taste

Lemon Chia Dressing
- 1 lemon (peel and all if organic)
- 2 tsps. chia seeds
- 1 clove garlic
- ½ cup soaked cashews
- 1 cup water
- ½ tsp oregano
- 1 tbsp. fresh dill
- pinch of black pepper
- ½ tsp. turmeric
- sea salt to taste

Basil Garlic Dressing
- ½ cup olive oil
- 2 tbsps. raw apple cider vinegar
- juice of 1 lemon
- 2 clove garlic
- 10 basil leaves
- sea salt to taste

Cherimoya Dressing
- fruit of 1 cherimoya
- juice of 2 lemons
- 2 dried pitted medjool dates
- 1 clove garlic
- 1 tbsp. dried basil
- 1 tbsp. dried dill
- 1 tbsp. dried parsley

Lemon Garlic Cashew Dressing
- ⅔ cup soaked cashews
- 1 clove garlic
- ½ lemon (peel and all if organic)
- 1 tbsp. onion powder
- 2 tbsps. olive oil
- ¾ cup water
- sea salt to taste

Simply Spicy & Delicious
- 1 large or 2 medium heirloom tomatoes
- small chunk of red onion
- ½ serrano pepper
- 15-20 soaked almonds
- sea salt to taste

Heaven on Earth
- 20 to 30 fresh chives
- 1 medium heirloom tomato
- 1 avocado
- Squeeze of fresh lemon
- sea salt to taste

Keep it Coming
- ½ cup olive oil
- 1 tsp. of chlorella
- 1 tsp. of spirulina
- 1 avocado
- 1 tbsp. raw apple cider vinegar
- pink Himalayan salt to taste

Anytime Blend
- 2 cups cherry tomatoes
- ⅓ cup of fresh basil
- 1 small red onion
- ¼ cup of raw organic apple cider vinegar
- sea salt to taste

Too Good
- 1/2 cup hemp seed oil
- 1 whole lemon (peel and all if organic)
- soaked sunflower seeds
- soaked pumpkin seeds
- sea salt to taste

Orange Pistachio Dressing
- 3 cups orange juice
- ¼ cup raw sesame seeds
- ¼ cup pistachios
- ¼ cup chives
- squeeze of lime juice
- 1 thumb-sized chunk of turmeric root
- sea salt to taste

Salads

Summertime Specialty
- red leaf lettuce
- 1 persimmon
- 10 sprigs of cilantro
- red onion
- broccoli
- radishes
- orange bell pepper
- lemon juice
- raw organic cold-pressed olive oil
- sea salt

Green Spirit
- romaine lettuce
- endive
- carrot
- heirloom tomato
- soaked jungle peanuts
- hemp oil
- fresh lime juice
- hawaiian sea salt
- spirulina powder

Farmer's Delight
- lacinato kale
- red leaf swiss chard
- asparagus
- cayenne pepper
- 1 avocado
- pistachio nut butter
- flax seed oil
- fresh squeezed orange
- chlorella powder

The Feast
- spinach
- broccoli
- yellow bell pepper
- green onion
- pili nut butter
- soaked walnuts
- raw organic apple cider vinegar
- raw organic cold-pressed olive oil
- pink Himalayan salt

The Bitter Sweet
- dandelion greens
- curly kale
- cauliflower
- leek
- celery
- cashew nut butter
- soaked pecans
- sacha inchi oil
- sea salt

Green Dream
- bok choy
- cucumber
- yellow bell pepper
- zucchini
- almond butter
- brazil nut butter
- chlorella tablets
- spirulina tablets
- walnut oil
- kala namak salt

Rainbow Blend
- rainbow swiss chard
- brussel sprouts
- beet
- orange bell pepper
- soaked pumpkin seeds
- soaked macadamia nuts
- hemp powder
- raw sesame oil
- raw apple cider vinegar
- pink himalayan salt

Wild Blend
- romaine lettuce
- 1 avocado
- dandelion greens and flowers
- chives
- spirulina tablets
- pink Himalayan salt

Summertime Favorite
- spinach
- 1 avocado
- broccoli
- red onion
- heirloom tomato
- chlorella tablets
- sea salt

Wonders of the World
- organic spring salad mix
- 4 leaves kale
- 1 avocado
- soaked sunflower seeds
- broccoli
- red onion
- heirloom tomato
- hemp seed oil
- olive oil
- lemon juice
- pink Himalayan salt

Helping Healer
- spinach
- romaine lettuce
- 1 avocado
- soaked walnuts
- soaked pumpkin seeds
- cucumber
- celery
- olive oil
- hemp seed oil
- sea salt
- spirulina powder

Hot Mess
- swiss chard
- 1 avocado
- soaked almonds
- asparagus
- jalapeno pepper
- cauliflower
- hemp seed oil
- olive oil
- sea salt
- chlorella powder

The Simple Life
- romaine lettuce
- 1 avocado
- grape tomatoes
- freshly milled flax seeds

sea salt

Wraps

Sea Bliss Wrap
- nori sheet
- ½ avocado
- wakame flakes (soak for at least 15 minutes)
- broccoli sprouts
- wild strawberry leaves
- fresh oregano
- pink Himalayan salt

Black Maple
- collard green
- ½ avocado
- nori flakes (soak for at least 15 minutes)
- black quinoa sprouts
- wild maple leaves
- fresh thyme
- sea salt

Iodinized
- grape leaves (I generally make 3 or 4 small wraps)
- ½ avocado
- dulse flakes (soak for at least 15 minutes)
- kombu flakes (soak for at least 15 minutes)
- alfalfa sprouts
- mugwort leaves
- sea salt

Swiss Bliss
- swiss chard (destemmed)
- ½ avocado
- arame flakes (soak for at least 15 minutes)
- azuki sprouts
- chick pea sprouts
- lovage leaf
- pink Himalayan salt

The Classic
- cabbage (destemmed)
- avocado
- carrot
- red onion
- tomato
- hemp seed oil
- sea salt

Lip Licker
- collard leaf (destemmed)
- avocado
- cayenne pepper
- diced celery
- diced cucumber
- kala namak salt

Tummy Tuck
- romaine lettuce
- avocado
- beet
- broccoli sprouts
- soaked sunflower seeds
- freshly squeezed grapefruit juice
- sea salt

Slap your Granny
- swiss chard (destemmed)
- avocado
- radish
- cauliflower
- soaked raw pumpkin seeds
- sacha inchi oil
- pink Himalayan salt

Veganism
- nori sheet
- avocado
- spinach
- sweet corn
- sweet peas
- hemp seed oil
- sea salt

The Boss
- kale (destemmed)
- bell pepper
- soaked raw almonds
- cashew butter
- raw organic apple cider vinegar
- pink Himalayan salt

Fermented Foods

Sauerkraut

- Cut one head of your favorite cabbage up into thin edible strips (about 2 lbs.)
- Rub 2 tablespoons of salt into the cut up vegetable
- Put salted cabbage into a jar with a tablespoon of caraway seeds
- Next put another jar, upside down, into the first jar with a cheese cloth over everything so that nothing enters the batch
- Weigh the jar down so that pressure keeps the cabbage together
- Within an hour the cabbage should be submerged in its own juice
- Taste test every few days until it is ready to go in the fridge

Enjoy!

Coconut Yogurt

- cut the top off of a coconut or and drain into your blender
- scrape the meat into the blender
- add 2 to 3 cups of your favorite soaked nuts or seeds
- add a live strain of probiotics
- blend and put in a mason jar and leave the lid slightly open
- let it set out for about two hours then and then put it in the fridge
- Let sit in the fridge for at least 24 hours to allow the bacteria to colonize
- consume within a week
- Optional add ins: your favorite fruits or superfood powders

Add to smoothies, dressings, or indulge with a spoon!

Enjoy!

Kombucha

- Things you will need include: a gallon glass jug, cheese cloth, a rubber band, a Kombucha starter culture, 10 bags of black tea, a wooden spoon, a pot to boil water, and a cup of raw organic cane sugar
- Start by boiling water
- Let tea sit and brew for twenty minutes
- Stir in sugar
- Let tea cool and put in culture
- Cover with cheese cloth and wrap with rubber band
- Let it sit out for several weeks or until taste is satisfactory
- Refrigeration stops the fermentation process

You can also add your favorite fruit to give your Kombucha additional flavors or experiment using different teas!

Enjoy!

Kimchi

- 2 lbs. cabbage
- 1 medium apple
- 1 small chopped red onion
- 2 cloves garlic
- 1 tbsp. cayenne powder
- ¼ cup pink Himalayan Salt
- 6 cups water

Directions: Cut cabbage up into appropriate bite-sized pieces. Put it in a bowl after this is completed with the salt and 2 cups of warm water. Mix it well with your hands and let it sit for at least two hours, up to 12. While this is soaking blend the rest of the ingredients including the four cups of reserved water. Drain off the cabbage brine into another bowl or cup. Add blended mixture to cabbage with one cup of brine from the drained liquid. Mix together well. Add to mason jars. Add more brine if necessary so that all cabbage is covered. Cover your jars with cheese cloth for one to four days. Try it periodically until you find the desired taste you enjoy. Once you do, seal the mixtures and put them in the refrigerator. Consume within two months.

Enjoy!

Gourmet Recipes

Rawghetti

- 1 to 3 zucchini depending on the size
- 1 ¼ cup grape tomatoes
- ½ yellow bell pepper
- 2 cloves garlic
- 2 tablespoons chopped red onion
- 5 to 7 fresh basil leaves
- 4 tablespoons olive oil
- sea salt to taste

Prepare zucchini by cutting of both ends. Using a vegetable peeler (or preferably a spiralizer) turn your zucchini into spaghetti strips (leave the skin on if organic). In a big bowl stir in zucchini with 1 tablespoon of olive oil and a pinch or two of sea salt. Blend the remaining ingredients in a blender until a chunky even consistency is reached. If your sauce is too thick for your liking I recommend adding more grape tomatoes or a ¼ cup water. Before enjoying this delicious meal, sprinkle with sea salt, nutritional yeast, and hemp seeds!

Serves: 1 to 3.

Raw Burgers

- 8 pieces romaine lettuce
- 1 avocado
- ¾ cup brazil nuts
- 4 slices red onion
- 2 medium-sized heirloom tomatoes
- ½ cucumber
- 2 teaspoons pink Himalayan salt
- 15-20 halved grape tomatoes

Take 1 pieces of lettuce for each side of your "bun". Fold both pieces in half and press them firm against a table so that the lettuce breaks to form an even surface. You will be making 4 sandwiches. Using a food processor or high speed blender, mix the avocado, brazil nuts, and salt. Evenly disperse the mixture onto the four slices, and place the grape tomatoes on top. Slice and add your desired amount of toppings. Enjoy!

Serves: 2.

Raw Sweet Onion Potato Bread

- 2 pounds of peeled sweet onions
- 3 peeled red potatoes
- 1 cup chia seeds
- 1 cup pumpkin seeds
- ⅓ cup olive oil
- 1 teaspoon sea salt

First start by blending or milling the pumpkin seeds and chia seeds. Put in a bowl with the olive oil and salt. Use a food processor for the onions and potatoes, or cut them into pea-sized pieces with a knife. Mix all the ingredients together. It should form a thick paste-like substance, if not simply add a tablespoon of water or olive oil. Using a dehydrator, heat between 100 to 105 degrees for 6 to 9 hours. This recipes typically yields between 3 to 4 trays of deliciousness. Flip your sheets of bread half way to achieve an even consistency. ENJOY!

Serves: 5 to 7.

Rawza

In order to create raw pizza, it's necessary to first make the crusts. They can be stored in the freezer for several days in an airtight bag or container.

- 1 ½ cup almonds
- ½ cup brazil nuts
- 1 cup chia seeds
- 1 cup water
- 2 tablespoons olive oil
- 1 tablespoon dried basil
- 1 tablespoon dried rosemary
- 1 tablespoon dried oregano
- 1 teaspoon of pink Himalayan salt

First, mill all the nuts and seeds in a food processor or high powered blender until they are a flour-like substance. Mix the rest of the ingredients in a bowl together with your ground up nuts and seeds. Shape your crusts on a dehydrator tray coated with coconut oil, but don't make them more than ⅜ inch thick. Dehydrate at 105 degrees for 9 to 13 hours. Now it's time to make the sauce!

- 3 cups tomatoes
- 10 dried tomatoes (soak overnight)
- 2 dried and pitted dates (soak overnight)
- ¼ inch slice of red onion
- ½ cup olive oil
- 2 tablespoons dried parsley

- 4 cloves garlic
- ¼ teaspoon cayenne (optional)
- 1 teaspoon pink Himalayan salt

Mix to an even consistency using a food processor or high speed blender, then spread on your crusts. Top with nutritional yeast and your favorite pizza toppings! Eat right away or heat in the dehydrator!

Serves: 2 to 3.

Raw Lasagne

Cheese Sauce:
- 2 cups soaked macadamia nuts
- 1 cup soaked cashews
- 2 tbsps. lemon
- 2 tbsps. nutritional yeast
- 1 orange bell pepper
- 2 tbsps. fresh parsley
- 1 tbsp. fresh thyme
- ½ tsp. sea salt
- ½ cup water

Blend and set said or put in refrigerator.

Meat Layer:
- ½ cup soaked walnuts
- 1 cup soaked sun dried tomatoes
- 2 tsps. oregano
- 2 tsps. sage
- ½ tsp. sea salt
- 1 tbsp. pine nuts

Process ingredients leaving it slightly chunky.

Tomato Sauce:
- 1 ½ cups soaked sun dried tomatoes
- 2 pitted dried medjool dates
- 2 cloves garlic
- 1 large heirloom tomato
- 1 tbsp. oregano
- 2 tbsps. olive oil
- 2 tbsps. lemon juice

Blend until smooth.

Pesto:
- 2 cups basil leaves
- ¾ cup pine nuts
- 3 tbsps. hemp seed oil
- 1 clove garlic
- 1 tbsp. lemon juice
- ½ tsp. salt

Process ingredients leaving it slightly chunky.

Spinach Layer:
- 6 cups torn layer
- 5 tbsps. oregano
- 1 tsp. olive oil
- ¼ tsp. sea salt

Mix ingredients in a bowl and let sit for 1 hour.

Pasta Layer:
- 5 zucchinis cut lengthwise into thin strips
- ½ tsp olive oil
- pinch of black or cayenne pepper
- 5 leaves of chopped basil

Marinate for 10 minutes.

Assembly:
Line the bottom of your pan or glass with half of the zucchini strips. Then add a layer of half of the meat layer, all the cheese, all the tomato sauce, and followed by all of the pesto.

Add the rest of the meat layer, followed by the entire spinach layer, and top it off with the rest of the zucchini pasta. Although it is not necessary you can refrigerate or dehydrate your raw lasagna to firm it up a little bit which will make it easier to cut. This recipe serves 8 to 10.

Enjoy!

Alfredo Pasta

Sauce:
- 2 cups chopped parsnips
- 2 cloves garlic
- 3 fresh sage leaves
- 1 tsp. thyme
- 1 tbsp. cashew butter
- ½ cup nutritional yeast
- ¼ cup walnut butter
- 1 cup water
- sea salt to taste

Blend until smooth!

For the pasta spiralize 6 cups of parsnips or zucchini. Add 2 cups of sliced crimini mushrooms, ½ small chopped red onion and 2 tbsps. chopped fresh sage.

Serves: 1 or 2.

Enjoy!

Printed in Great Britain
by Amazon